T 404003

Land of Liberty

New Mexico

by Kim Covert

Consultant:
Bárbara O. Reyes
Assistant Professor of History
University of New Mexico
Albuquerque, New Mexico

Capstone press

Mankato, Minnesota

Capstone Press
151 Good Counsel Drive • P.O. Box 669 • Mankato, Minnesota 56002
http://www.capstone-press.com
Copyright © 2004 by Capstone Press. All rights reserved.
No part of this publication may be reproduced in whole or in part, or stored in a retrieval system, or transmitted in any form or by any means, electronic, mechanical, photocopying, recording, or otherwise, without written permission of the publisher.
For information regarding permission, write to Capstone Press,
151 Good Counsel Drive, P.O. Box 669, Dept. R, Mankato, Minnesota 56002.
Printed in the United States of America

Library of Congress Cataloging-in-Publication Data
Covert, Kim.
　　New Mexico / by Kim Covert.
　　p. cm.—(Land of liberty)
　　Includes bibliographical references and index.
　　Contents: About New Mexico—Land, climate, and wildlife—History of New Mexico—Government and politics—Economy and resources—People and culture.
　　ISBN 0-7368-2189-9 (hardcover)
　　1. New Mexico—Juvenile literature. [1. New Mexico.] I. Title. II. Series.
F796.3.C687 2004
978.9—dc21　　　　　　　　　　　　　　　　　　　　　　　　　　2003000055

Summary: An introduction to the geography, history, government, politics, economy, resources, people, and culture of New Mexico, including maps, charts, and a recipe.

Editorial Credits
Erika L. Shores, editor; Jennifer Schonborn, series designer; Linda Clavel, book designer and illustrator; Enoch Peterson, illustrator; Jo Miller, photo researcher; Eric Kudalis, product planning editor

Photo Credits
Cover images: Pueblo near Taos, New Mexico, Tom Till; White Sands National Monument, Houserstock/Ellen Barone

Capstone Press/Gary Sundermeyer, 54; Corbis, 29; Corbis/Bettman, 26–27; Corbis/David Muench, 14; Corbis/Macduff Everton, 42–43; Corbis Sygma/Pat Cunningham, 36; Creatas, 57; Digital Vision Ltd., 23; Folio Inc./David R. Frazier, 46; Folio Inc./Richard Cummings, 18, 38; Getty Images/Hulton Archive, 24, 25; Houserstock/Dave G. Houser, 17; Houserstock/Ellen Barone, 41; Houserstock/Jan Butchofsky, 8; Linda Clavel, 52; North Wind Picture Archives, 20, 58; One Mile Up Inc., 55 (both); Pat & Chuck Blackley, 63; Photo courtesy of The Whole Enchilada Fiesta, Terry Guaderrama–photographer, 44; PhotoDisc Inc., 1; The Viesti Collection Inc./Joe Viesti, 50–51; The Viesti Collection Inc./Richard Cummins, 12–13; Tom Till, 49; U.S. Postal Service, 59; Visuals Unlimited/Joe McDonald, 16; Visuals Unlimited/Mark E. Gibson, 30; Visuals Unlimited/Mark S. Skalny, 56; Visuals Unlimited/Richard Thom, 4; Woodfin Camp & Associates Inc., 35

Artistic Effects
Comstock, Image Ideas/Comstock, Linda Clavel, PhotoDisc Inc.

1 2 3 4 5 6 08 07 06 05 04 03

Table of Contents

Chapter 1	About New Mexico	5
Chapter 2	Land, Climate, and Wildlife	9
Chapter 3	History of New Mexico	19
Chapter 4	Government and Politics	31
Chapter 5	Economy and Resources	39
Chapter 6	People and Culture	45
Maps	New Mexico's Cities	7
	New Mexico's Land Features	11
Features	Recipe: Biscochitos	54
	New Mexico's Flag and Seal	55
	Almanac	56
	Timeline	58
	Words to Know	60
	To Learn More	61
	Internet Sites	61
	Places to Write and Visit	62
	Index	64

Huge rock formations called stalactites and stalagmites are common in Carlsbad Caverns.

Chapter 1

About New Mexico

Visitors walk along a steep, slippery, and winding trail. They carefully make their way through a long tunnel that drops 750 feet (229 meters) under the ground. After walking about 1 mile (2 kilometers), they reach the Big Room. These visitors are in one of the caves of Carlsbad Caverns National Park. The Big Room is the largest cave in North America. It is more than 8.2 acres (3.3 hectares) in size. Six football fields could fit into the Big Room.

Carlsbad Caverns National Park is a series of 94 caves in southeastern New Mexico. Fantastic rock formations called stalactites hang down from the cave ceilings. Stalagmite columns rise up from the cave floors. These rocket-shaped formations

> **Did you know...?**
> The northwestern corner of New Mexico is part of the Four Corners. At this spot, New Mexico's border touches the borders of Utah, Colorado, and Arizona. The Four Corners is the only place in the nation where four states meet.

have names such as Temple of the Sun, Rock of Ages, and Giant Dome.

Jim White first explored Carlsbad Caverns in 1901. White discovered the caves after watching thousands of bats fly out of an opening in the ground.

Today, visitors can watch the bats leave the caves' entrance each night. Between 500,000 and 3 million Mexican free-tailed bats live in the caves from June through October. During winter, the bats live in Mexico.

The Land of Enchantment

New Mexico is called the Land of Enchantment because of its rich history and scenic beauty. The state has features to enchant, or charm, almost everyone. Nature lovers enjoy its mountains, deserts, and forests. Others value its American Indian villages, Spanish-style houses, and historical sites. New Mexico is a combination of Spanish, American Indian, and North American influences.

New Mexico is in the southwestern United States. Colorado borders it on the north. Oklahoma and Texas lie to the east. Arizona lies to the west, and Texas and Mexico are to the south.

Pine trees and colorful flowers grow in many parts of New Mexico.

Chapter 2

Land, Climate, and Wildlife

When artist Georgia O'Keefe came to New Mexico in 1929, she was inspired by the state's beautiful landscape. She saw some of the flattest land in the world and also some of the most rugged mountains. O'Keefe enjoyed the bright colors of the state's pine forests, green meadows, and mountain streams. O'Keefe later moved to New Mexico, where she painted colorful artwork featuring the state's deserts and mountain cliffs.

The land that inspired O'Keefe can be divided into four main regions. The Rocky Mountains and the Colorado Plateau cover northern areas of New Mexico. The Basin and Range Region is in southern New Mexico. The Great Plains covers the eastern third of the state.

The Rocky Mountains

The Rocky Mountains enter north-central New Mexico from Colorado. They stretch southward into New Mexico for about 120 miles (190 kilometers). The Rio Grande flows south between ranges of the Rocky Mountains. It is New Mexico's longest and most important river. The area surrounding the river creates the fertile Rio Grande valley.

The Rio Grande divides the state. To the east of the river is the Sangre de Cristo Range of the Rockies. The highest point in New Mexico, Wheeler Peak, is in this range. Wheeler Peak rises 13,161 feet (4,011 meters) above sea level. The Nacimiento and Jemez Mountain Ranges rise west of the Rio Grande. Forests of ponderosa pine, spruce, and aspen trees cover these mountains.

The Colorado Plateau

The Colorado Plateau covers northwestern New Mexico. This area has plains, valleys, deep canyons, and mesas. Mesas are flat-topped hills with steep sides.

A 40-mile (64-kilometer) strip of extinct volcanoes and lava plains are in the plateau area. This area is called El Malpais, which means "the badlands" in Spanish. El Malpais features a 17-mile (27-kilometer) lava tube. This tunnel of hardened lava lies below the surface of the lava plains.

New Mexico's Land Features

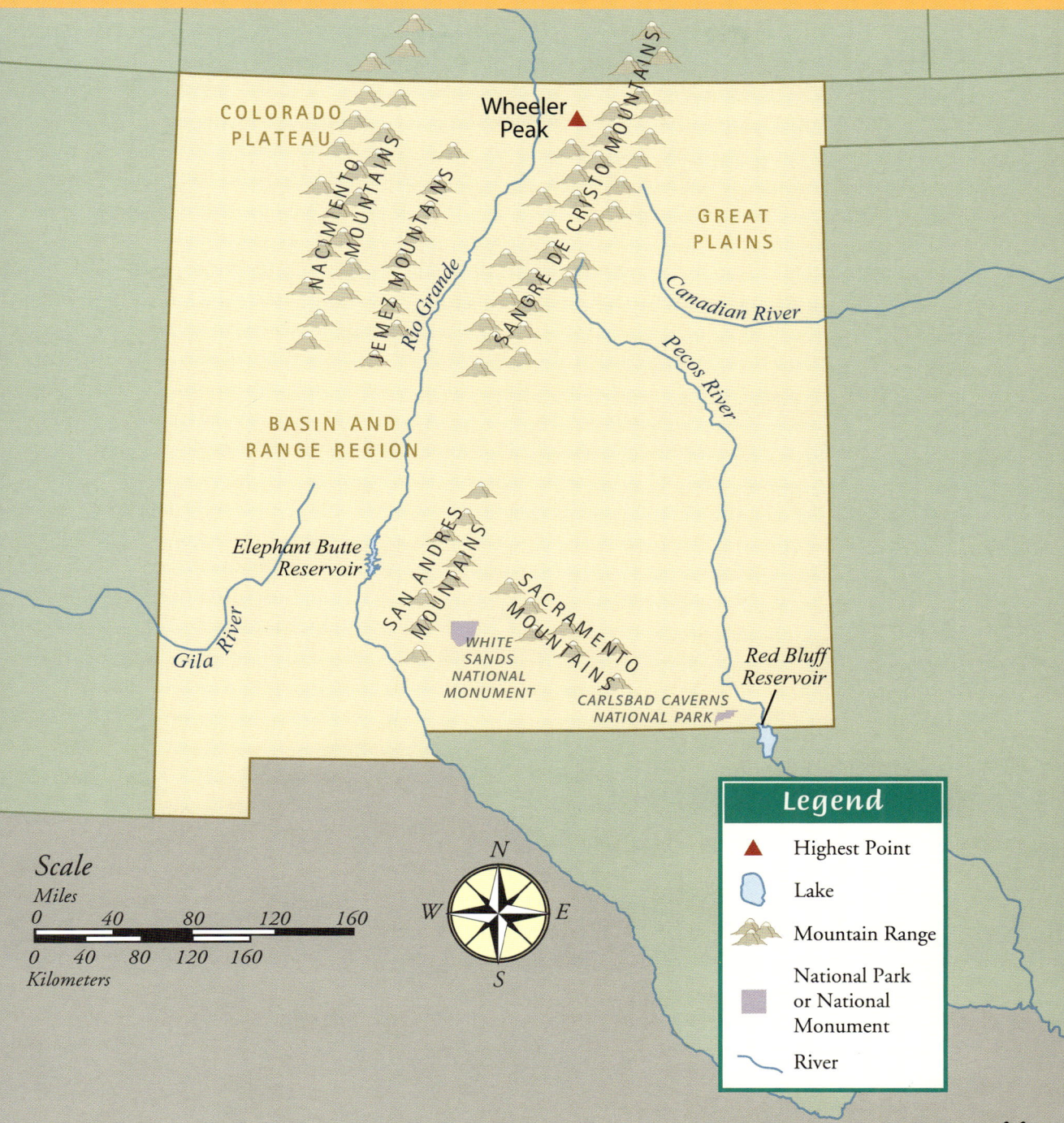

The Basin and Range Region

The Basin and Range Region extends south of the Rocky Mountains into southwestern New Mexico. Several mountain ranges are in this area. The Mogollon Mountains and Black Range are in the southwest.

Desert basins lie between the mountains in this region. The Tularosa Basin is the largest of these bowl-shaped valleys. It is between the Sacramento and San Andres Mountains. White sand dunes cover 275 square miles (712 square kilometers) of the basin. Gypsum crystals make up the white sand. This mineral is found in rocks in the mountains around

the basin. Winds constantly change the shape of the brilliant-white gypsum sand dunes. Some of the dunes rise 60 feet (18 meters) high.

The Chihuahuan Desert covers most of southwestern New Mexico. The Gila River runs west through the desert. Prickly pear and cholla cactuses grow there.

The Great Plains

The Great Plains covers the eastern third of the state. Grasslands grow on the northern part of this region. Sheep and cattle graze there. The Canadian River flows

In 1933, the U.S. government established White Sands National Monument to protect the desert area. It is the world's largest gypsum sand dune field.

Areas of high elevation, such as Sandia Peak in central New Mexico, receive the greatest amount of snowfall in the state.

east across the plains. To the west, the Pecos River flows through a wide valley.

The plains area south of the Canadian River is called the High Plains. The Spanish called it Llano Estacado, or Staked Plain. Some people believe early Spanish explorers placed wooden stakes in the ground to mark their way. They did not want to get lost on the vast, flat land.

The Red Bluff Reservoir is in southern New Mexico. It was formed by a dam on the Pecos River. It is the lowest point in New Mexico at 2,842 feet (866 meters) above sea level.

Climate

People enjoy New Mexico's climate. Summer days are hot. At night, the temperature drops. The average temperature in July is about 74 degrees Fahrenheit (23 degrees Celsius). The state's average temperature in January is 34 degrees Fahrenheit (1 degree Celsius). In January, temperatures are usually warmer in the south than in the north.

Precipitation amounts vary throughout the state. Little rain falls in south and central areas. These areas receive less than 10 inches (25 centimeters) a year. Higher mountain areas receive as much as 24 inches (61 centimeters) of precipitation annually. Snow falls throughout the entire state.

Wildlife

New Mexico is home to many types of wildlife. The mule deer, brown bear, mountain lion, and bobcat live in high mountain forests. Coyotes and jackrabbits live in lower regions. Many kinds of trout swim in mountain streams. About 300 types of birds live in New Mexico year round. Forty-six varieties of snakes live in New Mexico. Of these, the rattlesnake and the coral snake are venomous.

Peccaries eat the prickly pear cactus.

Roadrunners

New Mexico's state bird, the roadrunner, is a member of the cuckoo family. Roadrunners live in the deserts of the western United States. They have brown and white feathers, small wings, and long tails. Bushy feather crests stick up from their heads.

Roadrunners rarely fly, but they can run up to 15 miles (24 kilometers) per hour. They have long, strong legs. Their toes act like snowshoes to help them run across the desert sand. People often see roadrunners running along state highways.

One unique animal in New Mexico is the peccary. Peccaries are common in the southwestern part of the state. A peccary is the only wild, native, piglike animal found in the United States. The Spanish call the animal a jabalina or javelina. This name means "javelin," or "spear," in Spanish. Peccaries have very sharp tusks.

The ancient homes of New Mexico's earliest people have lasted for centuries.

Chapter 3

History of New Mexico

In 1926, scientists found stone spearheads near Folsom. These arrowheads show that American Indians hunted in northeastern New Mexico at least 10,000 years ago.

From about 500 B.C. to A.D. 1200, the Anasazi Indians lived in the San Juan River Basin in New Mexico. The Anasazi sometimes built large villages on top of mesas. They built some of their pueblos, or homes, five stories high. Some pueblos had more than 200 rooms.

By 1300, Pueblo Indians lived along the Rio Grande. The Pueblo are descendants of the Anasazi people. The Pueblo include the Zuni, Acoma, Hopi, and Rio Grande Indian groups.

In the 1530s, Álvar Núñez Cabeza de Vaca (far right) explored the area that is now New Mexico.

The Pueblo made pottery and blankets. Adobe bricks made of clay and straw were used to build Pueblo homes.

The Navajo and Apache Indians arrived in the area around the 1200s. They fought with the Pueblo Indians for hundreds of years. The Pueblo, Apache, Comanche, Navajo, and Ute peoples were in the New Mexico region when Spanish explorers arrived in the 1500s.

Spanish Rule

Spaniards were the first Europeans to arrive in New Mexico. In 1528, the Spanish explorer Álvar Núñez Cabeza de Vaca led a group of men west across Texas. After eight years, they reached the Rio Grande and New Spain. At that time, Spain owned present-day New Mexico and Mexico. Spain called the area New Spain.

Cabeza de Vaca returned to Mexico City, Mexico. He told Spanish officials about what he saw in the area that is now New Mexico. In 1538, officials sent Fray Marcos de Niza into the area explored by Cabeza de Vaca. When Marcos returned, he claimed to have seen the rich Seven Cities of Cíbola. These cities were believed to have gold and treasures.

In 1540, Francisco Vásquez de Coronado, with the help of Marcos, led an expedition into the area of New Mexico. Coronado discovered that the Seven Cities of Cíbola were actually Zuni and Hopi pueblos. He failed to find gold or other treasures and returned to Mexico.

Juan de Oñate founded the first European colony in New Mexico in 1598. Many Spaniards settled in San Juan.

In 1609, the king of Spain made New Mexico a royal colony. Pedro de Peralta became the first royal governor and established Santa Fe as the capital in 1610.

Roman Catholic priests often traveled with explorers and settlers. The priests set up missions to teach the American Indians to be Christians. The priests ruled these missions and punished people who did not practice Christianity.

In 1680, the Pueblo Indians forced the Spanish out of New Mexico. The Pueblo killed many Spanish colonists and priests and destroyed the missions.

In 1692, Diego de Vargas led the Spanish to conquer New Mexico again. The Pueblo Indians fought the Spanish for four years. When the Pueblo stopped fighting, colonists and priests returned to Santa Fe. For the next 125 years, the Spaniards and Pueblo Indians lived fairly peacefully in New Mexico.

Mexican Rule

In 1821, Mexico won its freedom from Spain. New Mexico then belonged to Mexico. The Mexican government wanted to trade goods with the United States. Thousands of Americans began trading with New Mexicans. Many traveled on El Camino Real or "The Royal Road" from Santa Fe to Chihuahua, Mexico.

In 1821, Captain William Becknell opened the Santa Fe Trail. This trail ran from Independence, Missouri, to Santa Fe. Traders on the trail brought goods from Missouri to New Mexico.

U.S. Territory

Soon, the U.S. government wanted all of the land in the southwest. This desire started the Mexican War (1846–1848). The U.S. Army took control of New Mexico. The Treaty of Guadalupe Hidalgo ended the war in 1848. It gave New Mexico and much of the West to the United States.

Mission churches such as this one were built in the early 1600s by Spanish priests.

Cattle Wars

In 1866, Texas longhorn cattle were brought to New Mexico. Large cattle ranches soon covered the plains. Many ranchers opened their own stores and banks. Ranchers competed for business. Often, the competition became violent.

One of these rivalries led to the Lincoln County War in 1878. The war began when a Lincoln County rancher hired gunmen to kill John Tunstall, a rival rancher and merchant. Tunstall's employees hired William Bonney, at right, to help them get even. Bonney was known as the outlaw Billy the Kid. Many fights took place between ranchers during the Lincoln County War. The Lincoln County sheriff killed Billy the Kid in 1881.

In 1850, Congress made New Mexico a territory. James C. Calhoun became the governor, and Santa Fe was the capital.

Between 1862 and 1864, Colonel Kit Carson led the New Mexicans in forcing both the Apache and the Navajo Indians to live on a reservation near the Pecos River. The Apache fought U.S. control for 20 years. The Apache leader Geronimo led many attacks against the U.S. troops.

In 1886, Geronimo finally surrendered. The U.S. government then forced Geronimo to move to Fort Sill in Oklahoma.

Economic Growth

Mining started in New Mexico in the 1800s. Gold was discovered in the Ortiz Mountains in 1828 and at Pino Altos in 1860. In 1869, miners discovered silver in the southwestern mountains. Elizabethtown and Silver City quickly grew as mining towns.

By 1880, railroads reached New Mexico's major cities. They brought thousands of settlers. Many settlers fenced the

Geronimo was an Apache warrior. He led many attacks on settlers and soldiers in Mexico and the southwestern United States in the 1870s and 1880s.

land and began farming. In most areas, there was not enough rain, and farmers had to irrigate their crops. They used canals and pipes to bring water from streams and rivers to their land.

Statehood

New Mexicans wanted to become a U.S. state. But many Americans were against statehood for the territory. They believed the settlers and Indians in New Mexico were uneducated lawbreakers. Others did not want a state with such a high number of Spanish-speaking people.

Finally, the U.S. government granted New Mexico statehood. On January 6, 1912, New Mexico became the 47th state. It had a population of about 330,000 people. The people elected William C. McDonald as the first state governor. Santa Fe became the state capital.

World War II

The United States entered World War II (1939–1945) in 1941. New Mexicans played an important role in helping the United States and its allies win the war.

During World War II, New Mexicans serving in the Philippines were captured by the Japanese as prisoners of war. The Japanese forced these soldiers to march across the Bataan Peninsula. Many prisoners became ill or died during the march.

> **Did you know...?**
> Many Navajo men fought in the Pacific as U.S. Marines in World War II. They developed a code in the Navajo language. The Navajo code talkers sent secret messages in this code. The Japanese could not break the code.

About 1,800 New Mexicans served in the Philippines at the beginning of the war. They were members of the 200th and 515th Coast Artillery units. After many battles, the Japanese defeated the units in 1942. They took the Americans as prisoners of war (POWs). The Japanese forced the POWs to march across the Philippines' Bataan Peninsula to prison camps. This event became known as the Bataan Death March. Many POWs died during the march or in the prison camps. About 900 POWs were released at the end of the war. In April 2002, the Bataan Memorial was completed in Albuquerque to honor the men of the 200th and 515th units.

In 1942, government scientists arrived at Los Alamos to work on the top-secret Manhattan Project. This project was to develop the atomic bomb. In July 1945, the government tested the first atomic bomb. It was exploded in the White Sands Desert near Alamogordo. In August, U.S. planes dropped two atomic bombs on Japan. The war ended when Japan surrendered.

Continued Growth

After the war, New Mexico grew as a research center and testing ground. Scientists at Los Alamos continued to study nuclear energy. White Sands Missile Range was created in 1945 to test rockets and weapons. In 1948, Sandia National Laboratories was established in Albuquerque to research weapons and work on military projects. Hundreds of highly-educated people came to the state to work on these projects.

In the 1990s, New Mexico increased its trade with Mexico. The North American Free Trade Agreement (NAFTA) started in 1994. This agreement made trading with Mexico easier. New Mexico's exports to Mexico increased by 33 percent in 1994.

On July 16, 1945, the first atomic bomb was tested in New Mexico's White Sands Desert.

New Mexico's legislature meets in the capitol building in Santa Fe.

Chapter 4

Government and Politics

Completed in 1966, New Mexico's capitol building in Santa Fe represents the state's American Indian culture. The capitol building is modeled after the Pueblo Indians' adobe-style architecture. The round building looks like the ancient Zia Indian symbol for the sun.

New Mexico's governor and lawmakers meet at the capitol. They work to improve the lives of New Mexico's people.

State Constitution

New Mexico adopted its constitution in 1911, one year before becoming a state. The constitution has been amended more than 100 times. A majority of New Mexican voters must

Did you know...?
Former governor Gary Johnson was the first governor to compete in Hawaii's Ironman World Championship Triathlon. Governor Johnson competed in 1993, 1997, and 1999. His best time in the swimming, biking, and running event was 10 hours, 39 minutes, and 16 seconds.

approve the amendments. Amendments affecting the voting rights and education of Spanish-speaking people have special procedures. English and Spanish are both official languages of New Mexico. New Mexico works to protect the rights of its Spanish-speaking citizens.

Branches of Government

New Mexico's government has three branches. The executive branch makes sure that laws are carried out. The legislative branch makes laws. The judicial branch involves the court systems that explain the laws.

The governor leads the executive branch. New Mexico's governor chooses many of the state's directors and board members. These positions include people in charge of finance, tourism, health, and public safety. Other members of the executive branch are elected by voters. These members include

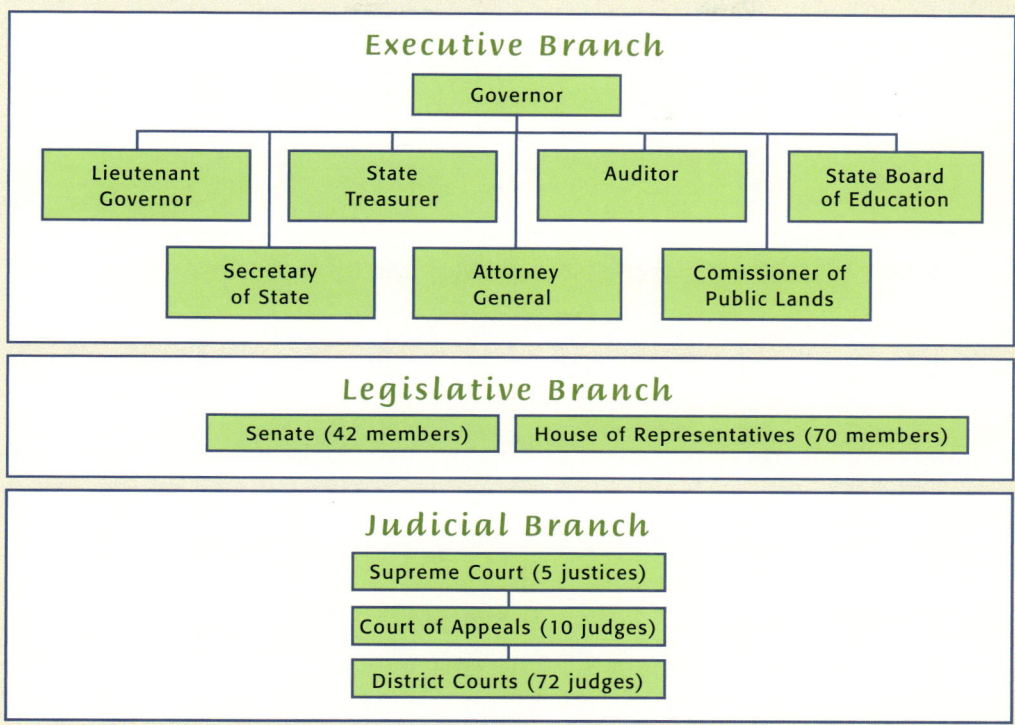

the lieutenant governor, secretary of state, state treasurer, auditor, attorney general, and commissioner of public lands.

All elected members of the executive branch serve four-year terms. They cannot serve more than two terms in a row. Governor Gary Johnson was elected in 1994 and again

> "The area is a part of who we are as a people and has a lot of meaning to my particular Pueblo and the Native American community. To have a road through the petroglyphs would be like putting a road through a church. That's what it means to us."
> —Stuwart Paisano, governor of the Sandia Pueblo, in 2002

in 1998. He was the first governor in the history of New Mexico to be elected to two four-year terms in a row.

The state legislature is made up of a senate and a house of representatives. The 42 senators are elected to four-year terms and the 70 representatives to two-year terms.

The court system makes up the judicial branch. New Mexico's courts have several levels. A person accused of committing a crime is usually first tried in a district court. The district court decides whether the person is guilty or innocent. A person found guilty can appeal the case to the court of appeals. The supreme court can hear appeals from the court of appeals. It has power over all of the other courts in the state.

In New Mexico, the Pueblo, Navajo, and Jicarilla and Mescalero Apache are self-governing nations. The 19 Pueblo communities each elect their own governors. They work together on the All Indian Pueblo Council. The Apache elect a president and vice president to lead their tribal council. An elected tribal council leads the Navajo Nation.

Blue Lake in northern New Mexico is sacred to the Taos Pueblo Indians.

The New Mexico State Office of Indian Affairs was created in 1953. It works to improve communication between the state government and the 22 tribal groups living in New Mexico.

During the 1900s, American Indians in New Mexico used the courts to gain some of their rights. The Pueblo worked for many years to regain their rights to Blue Lake. The U.S. government made the lake part of national forest lands in 1906.

Blue Lake is an important area to the Taos Pueblo religion. In 1970, the U.S. Congress gave the area back to the Pueblo.

State Challenges

New Mexico is one of the poorest states in the country. In 2000, about 18.4 percent of its people lived in poverty. Nearly half of New Mexico's American Indian population and 28 percent of Hispanics were at or below the poverty level. Many people do

U.S. Senator Pete Domenici has represented New Mexico in the U.S. Congress since 1973.

"We must put our state on a path to progress. We face daunting challenges—creating a high-wage economy, improving our schools, protecting our water and environment, providing adequate health care, providing clean energy."

—Governor Bill Richardson, January 21, 2003, state of the state address

not receive good health care. They do not have money to pay for health insurance.

In recent years, the state government has spent more money to provide better health care to the poor. It also has a welfare reform program. Low-income people can receive money from the government through this program. The programs help these people find work.

In 1986, New Mexico's U.S. Senators Pete Domenici and Jeff Bingaman founded a statewide plan called New Mexico First. People from around the state meet to discuss ways to solve New Mexico's problems. These people represent New Mexico's cultural, geographic, economic, and political diversity.

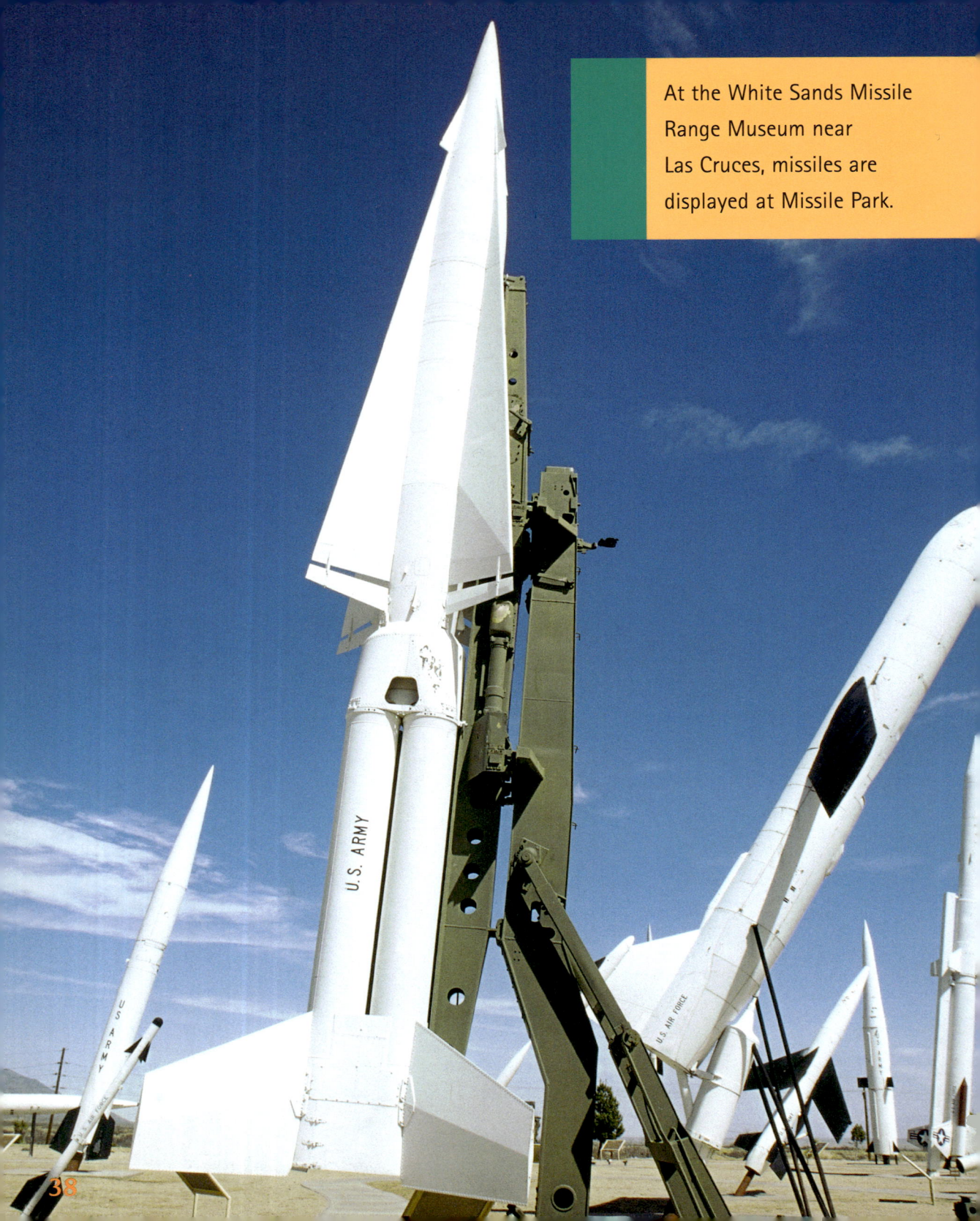
At the White Sands Missile Range Museum near Las Cruces, missiles are displayed at Missile Park.

Chapter 5

Economy and Resources

New Mexico has a diverse economy. Tourism, mining, and agriculture provide jobs for the state's workers. The government and scientific research companies also employ many New Mexicans.

Service Industries

Service industries provide the most money for New Mexico's economy. Service industries include government, tourism, health care, and retail stores.

Federal government research laboratories and military bases play a major role in the state's economy. Los Alamos National Laboratory is a world leader in nuclear energy research.

Sandia National Laboratories in Albuquerque is a leading center for nuclear weapons research. Military bases in New Mexico include Cannon Air Force Base, Kirtland Air Force Base, Holloman Air Force Base, and White Sands Missile Range.

Tourism is important to New Mexico's income. Millions of tourists visit New Mexico each year, producing more than $2 billion for the state's economy. Many visitors come to see the pueblos, historic sites, and American Indian cultural activities.

Manufacturing

New Mexico's leading manufactured products are computer and electronic equipment. Albuquerque is the state's leading manufacturing center. Two major electronics companies, Honeywell and Intel, have factories in the Albuquerque area. Honeywell makes military communication systems. Intel produces computer chips.

Other products manufactured in New Mexico include chemicals, clothing, food products, and petroleum products. Large oil refineries operate near Artesia, Farmington, and Gallup. These factories make gasoline and other products out of petroleum.

Roswell

In July 1947, something crashed near Roswell. At first, the U.S. Air Force said it was some type of aircraft from outer space. Many people panicked over this news. Later, the military said that it was a weather balloon. Many people, however, still believe the crashed object was an unidentified flying object (UFO). In 1991, the International UFO Museum and Research Center, at left, opened in Roswell.

Mining

New Mexico is one of the nation's leading mining states. Mining brings in almost $6 billion a year to the state's economy. The main mineral products are potash, uranium, coal, and copper. The state also leads the country in the production of perlite, which is used in making concrete, plaster, and potting soil.

New Mexico is the nation's top producer of potash, a mineral used in fertilizer. In 2000, New Mexico produced more than 70 percent of the nation's potash. Most of it comes from underground mines in southeastern New Mexico.

New Mexico is also a leading producer of uranium. This mineral is used in the production of nuclear energy. Most of New Mexico's uranium is mined in McKinley and Valencia Counties.

Agriculture

Agriculture is a valuable economic activity in New Mexico. New Mexico has about 16,000 farms and ranches. In 2000, ranching and farming added $2.1 billion to the state's economy.

Cattle ranching is New Mexico's leading agricultural activity. The state has about 1.7 million cattle. Ranchers raise beef cattle in almost every part of the state.

Crops are also important to New Mexico's agriculture. The state's leading crop is hay. New Mexico is also a leading state in the production of chile peppers and pecans. Other crops grown there include cotton, wheat, pinto beans, and lettuce.

Natural Resources

Water is New Mexico's most valuable resource. The state works hard to conserve its water. New Mexico and other western states have joined with Mexico to share the use of water from various streams and rivers.

Natural gas and petroleum are important natural resources in New Mexico. In 2000, New Mexico was the nation's third largest producer of natural gas. New Mexico sends much of its gas to other states through pipelines. Petroleum was first produced in 1909 from a well near Dayton. Petroleum is used to make gasoline. In 2000, New Mexico ranked sixth in the production of petroleum.

More than 6,000 cattle ranches are found throughout New Mexico. There are almost as many cattle in New Mexico as people.

Las Cruces hosts the Whole Enchilada Fiesta each fall. A parade and street party are part of the events.

Chapter 6

People and Culture

Every fall, Chef Roberto Estrada and his crew of 14 people in Las Cruces make the world's largest enchilada. Visitors to the Whole Enchilada Fiesta taste samples of this gigantic enchilada that weighs several thousand pounds and is 10 feet (3 meters) long. The Whole Enchilada Fiesta is one of New Mexico's traditions that celebrates the cultures of the state's diverse population.

American Indians, Hispanics, and Anglo-Americans all contribute to the state's culture. Hispanics are Spanish-speaking people of any nationality, but in New Mexico most Hispanics have Mexican backgrounds. Anglo-Americans, or Anglos, are

white people who do not have a Spanish background. New Mexico's three main ethnic groups influence its food, art, celebrations, and daily life.

Population

In 2000, New Mexico ranked 36th in population among the 50 states. Most New Mexicans live in the state's three largest areas, Albuquerque, Las Cruces, and Santa Fe. New Mexico's population increased 21 percent from 1990 to 2000.

The Taos Pueblo Indians continue to live in New Mexico.

New Mexico's Ethnic Backgrounds

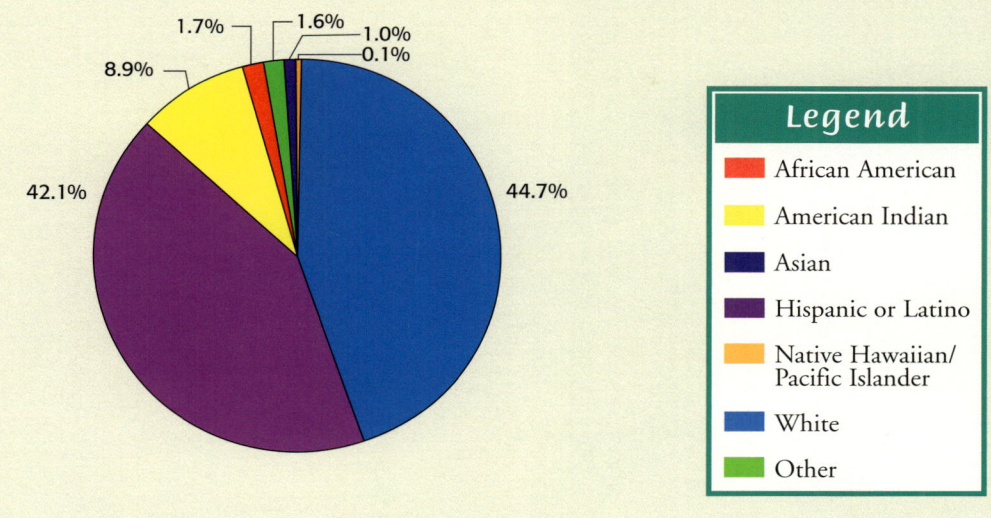

Today, most New Mexicans are descendants of the three main groups of people who settled the state. New Mexico has a higher percentage of American Indians and Hispanics than any other state.

American Indians

The Apache, Navajo, and Pueblo are the main American Indian groups living in New Mexico. Many live on the state's six reservations or in the 19 Pueblo villages.

> **Did you know...?**
> The New Mexico town of Truth or Consequences is named after a radio quiz program. In 1950, the town changed its name from Hot Springs. In exchange, the show broadcast one program from the town. Today, local people usually call the town "T or C."

Most Navajo live on a large reservation in northwestern New Mexico. Many Navajo raise sheep. They also work in oil and mineral production, manufacturing, and farming. Some Navajo earn money by making and selling traditional Navajo rugs.

The Pueblo people live in the western, northern, and central parts of the state. Most Pueblo villages are located in the Rio Grande valley. Many of the Pueblo people work at Los Alamos National Laboratory. Traditional arts and crafts also provide income for the Pueblos.

Two groups of Apache, the Jicarilla and the Mescalero, live on separate reservations. The Jicarilla live in northwestern New Mexico. Many Jicarilla people earn money by ranching and cutting lumber. The Mescalero live in south central New Mexico and work in lumbering and ranching. They also own the Ski Apache resort. This resort is the only ski area in the southern part of the state.

Sky City

Some Pueblo Indians live in a village called Sky City, at left. This village was built on a steep mesa that rises 357 feet (109 meters) above the plains. There are 250 dwellings in Sky City. People have lived in Sky City since 1150. It is considered to be the oldest inhabited village in the United States. Each Acoma Pueblo family owns one dwelling on the Sky City mesa, but only about 40 Acoma live in Sky City year-round. Many more come to Sky City for celebrations.

Hispanics and Anglos

El Camino Real was a major trade route between New Mexico and Mexico. People traveling the route brought many Spanish foods and traditions to the area. Most of the early settlers in the area were descendants of the Spaniards and Mexicans who moved north from Mexico. Today, less than one-third of New Mexico's population is of purely Spanish origin.

Anglo-Americans are the third group of the state's three main cultures. Many Anglo-Americans traveled west over the Santa Fe Trail. Some chose to settle in New Mexico. Today, Anglos live in most areas of the state. Most Anglos earn a living through a variety of jobs including ranching, mining, and service industries.

Celebrations

Each year, many cities in New Mexico host Spanish festivals, American Indian ceremonies, and other activities. Each October, the International Hot Air Balloon Festival in Albuquerque features about 1,000 colorful balloons that sail through the sky.

The city of Hatch calls itself the Chile Capital of the World. New Mexico leads the nation in the production of long green

and red chile peppers. Each fall, about 30,000 people visit Hatch to buy newly harvested chiles. The festival includes a parade, carnival, and contest for the best chile dish.

Pueblo Indians preserve traditional dances by performing at fiestas. The San Felipe Pueblo welcome visitors for their annual Green Corn Dance on May 1. In September, the Sun Dance takes place at Taos Pueblo's Fiesta of San Geronimo.

Art

Many writers and artists have lived in New Mexico. Author D. H. Lawrence lived in Taos. Pulitzer Prize-winning

Colorful balloons fill the sky at the annual International Hot Air Balloon Festival in Albuquerque. People from all over the United States come to watch.

The Inn at Loretto is in Santa Fe. This hotel displays the adobe style of architecture.

journalist Ernie Pyle lived in Albuquerque. Georgia O'Keefe, Bill Tate, Peter Hurd, and other famous artists also made their homes in New Mexico.

The architecture of New Mexico represents its three cultures. Spanish settlers made some changes to the style of Indian pueblo buildings when they built Santa Fe. This newer style is known as the Spanish mission style. Anglos brought new building materials and tools when the railroads came to

"In the magnificent fierce morning of New Mexico, one sprang awake, a new part of the soul woke up suddenly, and the old world gave way to a new."

—D. H. Lawrence, author, lived in Taos

New Mexico. Metal for roofs and glass for windows were added to the area's buildings.

Handcrafts are also important in New Mexico. Local Indians make unique pottery. Each village has its own design to identify the work of its people. Woven Navajo blankets are famous throughout the world. Many Indians make rings, necklaces, and belts to sell to tourists.

Recreation

New Mexico's scenery and outdoor activities attract visitors throughout the year. Many people enjoy rafting and kayaking on the Rio Grande. New Mexicans can hike and camp in the state's five national forests. The state has nine ski resorts for snowboarding and skiing.

Many people come to New Mexico to experience its rich history, cultural diversity, and beautiful scenery. For the people of New Mexico, these elements combine to make their state the Land of Enchantment.

Recipe: Biscochitos

In 1989, the New Mexico legislature adopted the biscochito as the official state cookie. New Mexico was the first state to have an official cookie. The biscochito is a traditional Spanish cookie made for special celebrations.

Ingredients

1 pound (455 grams) lard
1½ cups (360 mL) sugar
2 teaspoons (10 mL) anise seed
2 eggs, beaten
6 cups (1,440 mL) flour
1 tablespoon (15 mL) baking powder
1 teaspoon (5 mL) salt
½ cup (120 mL) white grape juice
¼ cup (60 mL) sugar
1 tablespoon (15 mL) cinnamon

Equipment

large mixing bowl
electric mixer
dry-ingredient measuring cups
measuring spoons
medium mixing bowl
liquid measuring cup
rolling pin
cookie cutter
baking sheets
small mixing bowl

What You Do

1. Preheat oven to 350°F (180°C).
2. In a large mixing bowl, use the electric mixer to soften the lard. Mix until fluffy.
3. Add 1½ cups (360 mL) sugar and anise seed and mix well.
4. Add beaten eggs and mix well.
5. Combine flour, baking powder, and salt in a medium mixing bowl.
6. Alternately add flour mixture and juice to the creamed mixture until the dough is stiff.
7. Mix dough slightly and pat or roll to about ½ inch (1.25 centimeters) thick.
8. Use a cookie cutter to cut the dough into shapes.
9. Place shapes on ungreased baking sheets.
10. Combine ¼ cup (60 mL) sugar and cinnamon in a small mixing bowl.
11. Sprinkle the top of each cookie with a small amount of the sugar mixture.
12. Bake for 10 minutes, or until cookies are lightly browned.

Makes about 3 dozen cookies

New Mexico's Flag and Seal

New Mexico's Flag

New Mexico adopted its flag in 1925. A red Zia symbol is in the center of the flag. The Zia is an ancient sun symbol of the Zia Indians. Four lines extend from each side of the circle. One group stands for north, south, east, and west. Another group of lines stands for the seasons of the year. Four lines represent the four parts of the day. Childhood, youth, middle years, and old age are represented by the last four lines.

New Mexico's State Seal

New Mexico adopted its state seal in 1913, one year after becoming a state. Two eagles are on the seal. The American bald eagle stands for the United States. The eagle holds three arrows in its claws. The eagle's wing shields a smaller Mexican brown eagle. This image represents the New Mexico Territory joining the United States. The brown eagle holds a cactus and snake. They stand for an ancient Aztec myth. A scroll below the eagles shows the state's motto, Crescit Eundo. This Latin phrase means "It grows as it goes."

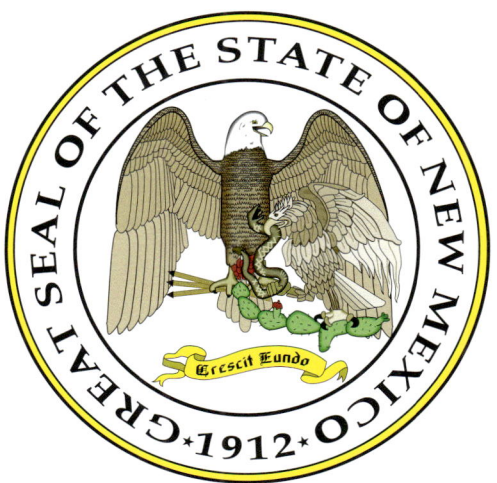

Almanac

General Facts

Nickname: Land of Enchantment

Population: 1,819,046 (U.S. Census 2000)
Population rank: 36th

Capital: Santa Fe

Largest cities: Albuquerque, Las Cruces, Santa Fe, Rio Rancho, Roswell

Geography

Area: 121,593 square miles (314,312 square kilometers)

Size rank: 5th

Highest point: Wheeler Peak, 13,161 feet (4,011 meters) above sea level

Lowest point: Red Bluff Reservoir, 2,842 (866 meters)

Agriculture

Agricultural products: Cattle, dairy products, sheep, hay, chile peppers, pecans

Climate

Average winter temperature: 34 degrees Fahrenheit (1 degree Celsius)

Average summer temperature: 71 degrees Fahrenheit (22 degrees Celsius)

Average annual precipitation: 13 inches (33 centimeters)

yucca flowers

black bear

Symbols

Animal: Black bear

Bird: Roadrunner

Cookie: Biscochito

Fish: Cutthroat trout

Symbols

Flower: Yucca

Gem: Turquoise

Insect: Tarantula hawk wasp

Motto: It grows as it goes

Song: "O, Fair New Mexico," by Elizabeth Garrett

Tree: Piñon

Economy

Natural resources: Uranium, potash, petroleum, natural gas, copper, lead

Types of industry: Tourism and other services, agriculture, manufacturing, mining

Government

First governor: William C. McDonald, 1912–1916

Statehood: January 6, 1912; 47th state

U.S. Representatives: 3

U.S. Senators: 2

U.S. electoral votes: 5

Counties: 33

57

Timeline

State History

1536
Spanish explorer Álvar Núñez Cabeza de Vaca enters New Mexico from Texas.

1540
Francisco Vásquez de Coronado explores New Mexico for Spain.

1821
Mexico wins its independence from Spain.

1848
The United States defeats Mexico in the Mexican War.

1850
The U.S. Congress creates the New Mexico Territory.

U.S. History

1620
The Pilgrims establish the Massachusetts Bay Colony.

1775–1783
The United States and Great Britain fight the Revolutionary War.

1812–1814
The United States fights Great Britain in the War of 1812.

1861–1865
Union states fight Confederate states in the Civil War.

1912
On January 6, New Mexico becomes the 47th state.

1945
The first atomic bomb explodes in the White Sands Desert.

1994
The North American Free Trade Agreement increases trade between New Mexico and Mexico.

1939–1945
World War II is fought; the United States enters in 1941.

1914–1918
World War I is fought; the United States enters the war in 1917.

1964
The Civil Rights Act is passed, which makes discrimination illegal.

2001
Terrorists attack the World Trade Center and the Pentagon on September 11.

Places to Write and Visit

Carlsbad Caverns National Park
3225 National Parks Highway
Carlsbad, NM 88220

International UFO Museum and Research Center
114 N. Main Street
Roswell, NM 88202-2221

National Hispanic Cultural Center of New Mexico
1701 Fourth Street SW
Albuquerque, NM 87102

New Mexico Department of Tourism
491 Old Santa Fe Trail
Santa Fe, NM 87501

Office of the Governor
State Capitol
Room 400
Santa Fe, NM 87501

The rapids on the Rio Grande attract rafters.

Index

agriculture, 26, 39, 42, 43, 48
American Indians, 6, 19, 22, 26, 31, 34–36, 40, 45, 47–48, 50, 53
    Anasazi Indians, 19
    Apache Indians, 20, 24, 25, 34, 47, 48
    Navajo Indians, 20, 24, 28, 34, 47–48, 53
    Pueblo Indians, 19–22, 31, 34–36, 46, 47, 48, 49, 51
architecture, 6, 19–20, 31, 52–53
atomic bomb, 28, 29

Basin and Range Region, 9, 12–13
Bataan Death March, 27, 28
Billy the Kid. See Bonney, William
Bingaman, Jeff, 37
Black Range, 12
Bonney, William (Billy the Kid), 24

Calhoun, James C., 24
Camino Real, El, 22, 49
capitol, 30, 31
Carlsbad Caverns, 4, 5–6
Carson, Kit, 24
cattle wars, 24
celebrations, 44, 45, 46, 49, 50–51
climate, 14, 15
Colorado Plateau, 9, 10

Domenici, Pete, 36, 37
explorers, 15, 20–22
    Cabeza de Vaca, Álvar Núñez, 20, 21
    Coronado, Francisco Vásquez de, 21

Geronimo, 24–25
government, 30, 31–37, 39
Great Plains, 9, 13, 15

Jemez Mountains, 10

Llano Estacado, 15
Los Alamos National Laboratory, 39, 48

Malpais, El, 10
Manhattan Project, 28
manufacturing, 40, 48
Marcos, de Niza, Fray, 21
McDonald, William C., 27
Mexican War, 23
mining, 25, 39, 41, 50
missions, 22, 23
Mogollon Mountains, 12

Nacimiento Mountains, 10
natural resources, 43
North American Free Trade Agreement (NAFTA), 29

O'Keefe, Georgia, 9, 52
Oñate, Juan de, 21

Peralta, Pedro de, 22
population, 27, 45–47, 49
priests, 22, 23
pueblos, 19, 21, 40, 52

recreation, 53, 63
Red Bluff Reservoir, 15
Rio Grande, 10, 19, 21, 48, 53, 63
Rocky Mountains, 9–10, 12

Sacramento Mountains, 12
San Andres Mountains, 12
Sandia National Laboratories, 29, 40
Sangre de Cristo Range, 10
Santa Fe, 22, 23, 24, 27, 30, 31, 46, 52
Santa Fe Trail, 23, 49
Seven Cities of Cíbola, 21
Sky City, 49
stalactite, 4, 5–6
stalagmite, 4, 5–6
state flag, 55
statehood, 26–27
state seal, 55

tourism, 32, 39, 40
Treaty of Guadalupe Hidalgo, 23
Tularosa Basin, 12

Vargas, Diego de, 22

Wheeler Peak, 10
White, Jim, 6
White Sands Missile Range, 29, 38, 40
White Sands National Monument, 13
wildlife, 6, 16–17
World War II, 27–28